PENGUIN BOOKS

FALLING IN LOVE

Jacky Fleming went to a suffragette school in London. She emerged awesomely uneducated due to the teachers' inexplicable preference for Latin as a first language. A year at Chelsea School of Art and a degree in Fine Art at Leeds University greatly improved her table football technique. Other qualifications include A– for posture and a silver medal in Latin-American dancing. A brief stint in the art department of a London periodical was followed by eleven years teaching art as a foreign language. Jacky lives in Yorkshire and hates cooking.

Her cartoons have been published by the BBC, The Women's Press, Virago, Leeds Postcards, Longman, The Open University, *New Internationalist*, *Harpies and Quines*, *New Woman*, *M & M*, *Viva*, Headline and others. Penguin also publish her popular books of cartoons, *Be a Bloody Train Driver!* and *Never Give Up*.

JACKY FLEMING

Falling In Love

PENGUIN BOOKS

PENGUIN BOOKS

Published by the Penguin Group
Penguin Books Ltd, 27 Wrights Lane, London W8 5TZ, England
Penguin Books USA Inc., 375 Hudson Street, New York, New York 10014, USA
Penguin Books Australia Ltd, Ringwood, Victoria, Australia
Penguin Books Canada Ltd, 10 Alcorn Avenue, Toronto, Ontario, Canada M4V 3B2
Penguin Books (NZ) Ltd, 182–190 Wairau Road, Auckland 10, New Zealand

Penguin Books Ltd, Registered Offices: Harmondsworth, Middlesex, England

This collection first published in book form 1993
3 5 7 9 10 8 6 4 2

Printed in England by Clays Ltd, St Ives plc

For Crazy Daisy

Contents

Prologue

ha ha

Getting Bigger

When girls are very small – under three foot –
boys are not of particular interest, unless they
are also under three foot.

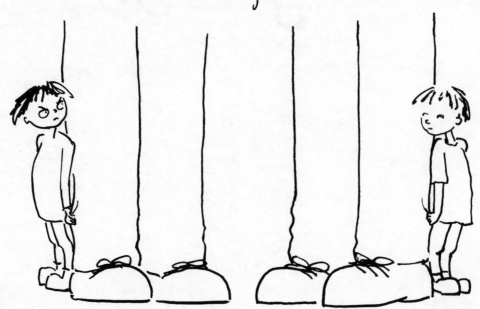

At this age girls are rightly suspicious that boys want what girls have got. Girls also want what boys have got as long as it's plastic and brightly coloured.

Otherwise they can keep it.

Both sexes manage to play amicably together without 'masculine' or 'feminine' behaviour emerging

much.

It is assumed by experts that young girls are consumed with envy when they discover that boys have a small protuberance which they haven't got.

what's that?

In fact all protuberances, light switches, worms, plug sockets, nipples, sweets, and kitchen appliances are equally fascinating

wierdy worm

but not worth building theories of gender difference upon.

Small girls will demonstrate an atavistic and ferocious attraction to petticoats, ribbons, lipstick, high heels and jewellery.

But so will boys given the chance.

At four foot six both sexes display a completely
uncalled for separatism and hostility towards each other

which if encouraged and rewarded could save
everybody a lot of trouble later on.

If they are fortunate they will progress easily from this stage into confident, self-possessed homosexuality, with the occasional foray into heterosexuality when they are old enough* to grasp the risks involved in such a move into alien territory.

tonight we will have passionate sex but tomorrow you must return to your own people

* 50 ish

If they are less fortunate they will go through a traumatic emotional transition to accommodate the supposedly natural attraction of the opposite sex. This involves a complete personality change which is particularly abhorrent to girls who quite rightly

smell a rat.

Whilst girls gather useful insights into their destiny

boys find that, on the whole, things are on their side . . .

unless they still pine for petticoats, ribbons, lipstick, high heels and jewellery, in which case things are not on their side at all.

...DISOWN you
...CUT you out of my will
...don't EVER let me catch you .....no son of mine
...DO I MAKE MYSELF CLEAR?

Girls can provoke the same disapproval by being adventurous, assertive, independent, strong-willed, angry, loud, messy, large, clever, witty, inquiring, having short hair, or being very good at football.

...LOOK at the state of you
NO way for a girl to behave
... dangerous..... tomboy
....what happened to that
nice dress I bought you?

Or a mere

can be sufficient to cause
Severely Restricted Expectations for the Future

Girls soon realise that what is expected is a quick turnabout in which they should attempt to become smaller, thinner, prettier, sillier, less resilient, irrational, spatially unaware, sentimental, insecure, dependent, meek, self-deprecating, emotionally attached to anything small and furry, and very bad at maths

silly me

for which they will be in some way rewarded.....

All other interests fall by the wayside, but this seems a small price to pay for... er... for... don't know really...

Before puberty girls achieve good results at school.
This stops when History, Science, English, French, Maths,
Biology, Sociology, Art, Music, Politics, Geography, Gym,
are replaced by Perpetual Anxiety About Looking Good.

this gives boys the
chance to catch up

and girls to get
various nervous disorders

Girls learn to encourage each other, as they are moulded and groomed for Love.

This is known as 'femininity.'

They become particularly prone to the following behaviour :

incessant non-specific yearning, extremely distorted perception (of men in particular),
overwhelming tolerance and compassion for appalling behaviour (of men in particular),
an inability to recognize what is damaging to self-respect (by men in particular),
and a compulsive attraction to seek out all of the above (with men in particular).

This is known as 'falling in love'.

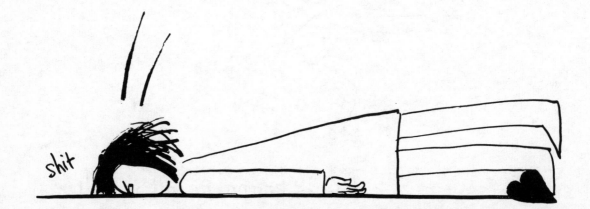

22

Getting Smaller

It is well known that Love is blind. In fact it is severely myopic which is not romantic but dangerous.

Friends will make futile, irritating attempts to point this out.

Our hearing is also severely distorted.
Everything he says is extraordinarily charming...

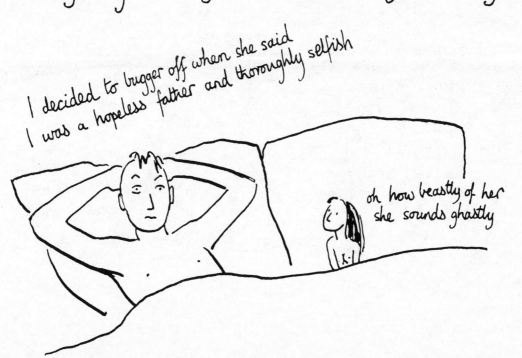

and only makes him more perfect.

The trouble is I'm honest to a fault.
Every time I had an affair I TOLD her
about it. I didn't HIDE anything or LIE

and she didn't appreciate it?
You SAINT

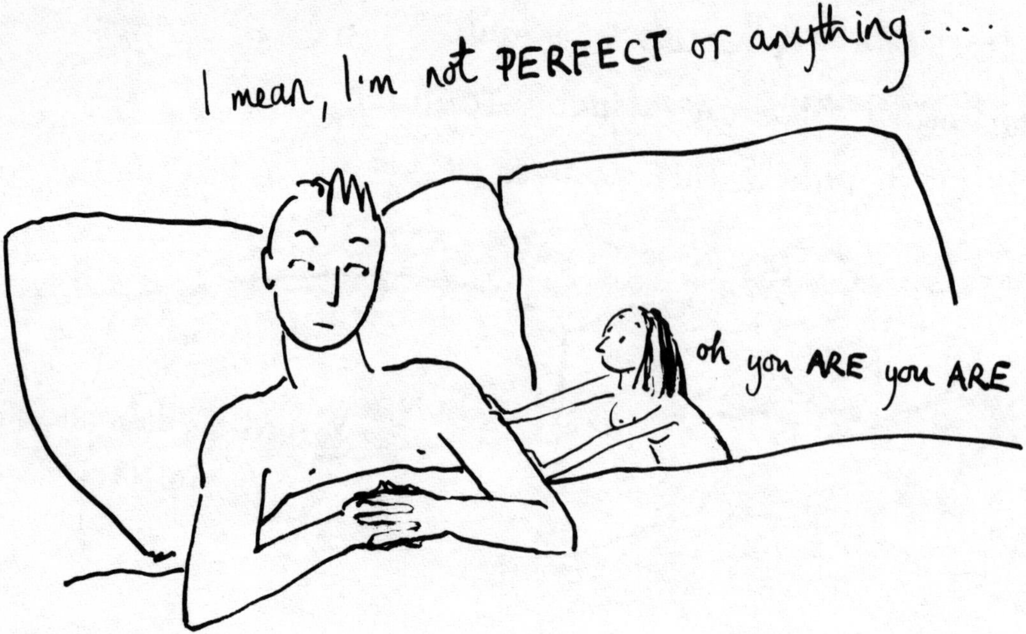
I mean, I'm not PERFECT or anything....
oh you ARE you ARE

Nothing can alter our distorted perception...

Well, not for long anyway.
Well, not for long ENOUGH anyway.

A lot of time has been spent on whether or not MEN are
The Answer, what SORT of man is The Answer, is he in fact
The Answer, would a shorter, chubbier, balder man have been
a BETTER Answer

when more attention should have been paid to The Question, which is : How Wrong Can a Girl Be? The answer is : Very.

how very?

Here are some questions to help you work out how very:

1. Prince Charming has finally seduced you despite some small reluctance on your part to have sex so soon. Next morning he behaves as though you proposed marriage in your sleep and backpeddles at a rate of knots, even though sex was sensational (you were anyway, he was OK).

DO YOU

a. *recognize a rat when you've slept with him and call it off.*
b. *fall hopelessly in love and pursue him desperately.*

a. **5 points for getting out while you can. Shame you didn't spot it sooner.**
b. **–79 points. Hopeless is the word. In the time you waste on him you could have qualified as a lawyer.**

2. Although Prince Charming originally fell for your independence, talent, and strength, you keep noticing that he subtly undermines your work, wants to drive you everywhere. and talks to you in a baby voice.

DO YOU

a. *recognize that he is frightened of women, terrified of strong women, deeply competitive and insecure, and call it off before you loose what you've got.*

b. *begin to doubt yourself and give him your car keys.*

a. 7 points for self-respect.

b. –200 points. IDIOT.

3. Prince Charming likes to think of himself as a sensitive man, but often says: 'It's all right for women. If a man did that he'd be called a sexist pig!'

DO YOU
a. *say men DO that extremely often and HAVE been doing it for an exceedingly long time without being called anything at all, and recognize him for the seething resentful misogynist he really is.*
b. *suspect he may have a point and stop calling yourself a feminist.*

a. **10 points. There's many a shit in sheep's clothing.**
b. **−380 points. You have just sold arms to the enemy.**

If you scored 22 we could all learn a thing or two from you. Please get in touch and write your own book.

If you scored –659 you may find Barbara Cartland more to your liking and you have probably started to twitch. At least your maths isn't too bad.

-79
-200 is er..
-279
-380 equals... er..
um.... -659

Men

There has been much discussion about the differences between the sexes. Usually the discussion gets stuck at first base on whether the differences are genetic or cultural.

I suspect that GENETICALLY I'm allergic to cleaning and CULTURALLY I need to have sex with a lot of people

Quite honestly, by the time you're living with him it doesn't make a great deal of difference.

However there are two differences worth bearing in mind
1. Men do exactly what they want
2. They don't feel bad about it

That's completely untrue.
I do exactly what I want
and if I get caught I
feel bad about it

There are also nice men who are never quite in focus,
always just off screen

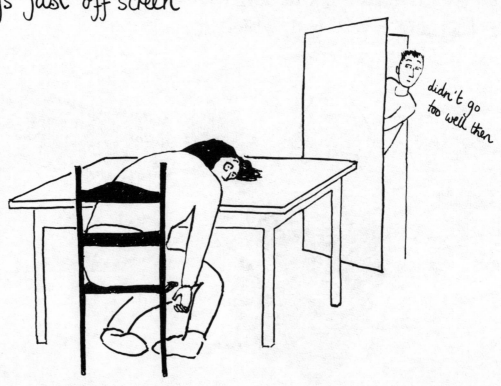

didn't go
too well then

the one who's just THERE for you, without being asked.

Or noticed.

There are also Opportunist Men who pose as nice men but will secretly make a list of everything they've done for you, because you OWE THEM

Never accept favours from this man. Ever.

Usually you can tell fairly early on if something's not quite right

actually I'm married but my wife doesn't understand me

How extraordinary. Which bit doesn't she understand? Your need for a bit on the side, your preference for home cooking, why she married you in the first place...

If you take over where his mother left off - BE WARNED

After many years of nurturing he may feel confident enough to leave home.

We have GOT to talk about the children.
I'm worried about Steven

Steven.....ah yes...
strange fellow with
the specs

When you do finally meet the only man in the world
who is courageous, humane, intelligent, witty, sensitive,
charming, sexy, imaginative, independent, single, filthy rich,
and had a vasectomy* your hormones will make you say

I can't BEAR his snoring
I can't BEAR his BREATHING
I can't BEAR the way he
SLEEPS lying DOWN

* this character is purely fictitious and any resemblance to any living person is highly unlikely

Sex

There is some confusion over which is sex and which is love but on the whole sex is less confusing than love, lust is less confusing than sex and chocolate is less confusing than any of them. Sex is when chocolate won't do.
Love is when sex won't do.
And lust is when almost anyone will do.
Chocolate is by far the safest bet in every respect but sex is by far the most interesting.
Love is what makes people forget to use contraceptives. Or is that sex? Anyway, love produces babies and then you can forget the sex and the lust.

Contrary to popular belief you will NOT discover everything you want to know about sex by going to the cinema.

IS THAT NICE?

well...QUITE nice.....
in an irritating
well-intentioned
sort of way

I'm probably asking the obvious but what are you doing exactly?

"Select the most attractive part of your body, and make sure it's visible throughout lovemaking."

multiple orgasms
are a MYTH
Geoffrey, a
MYTH

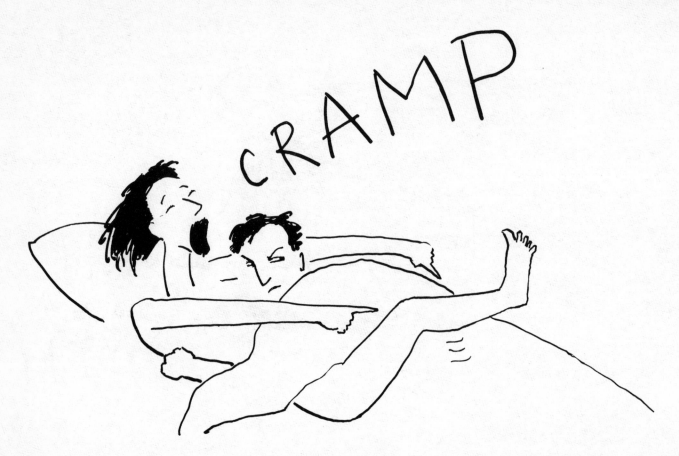

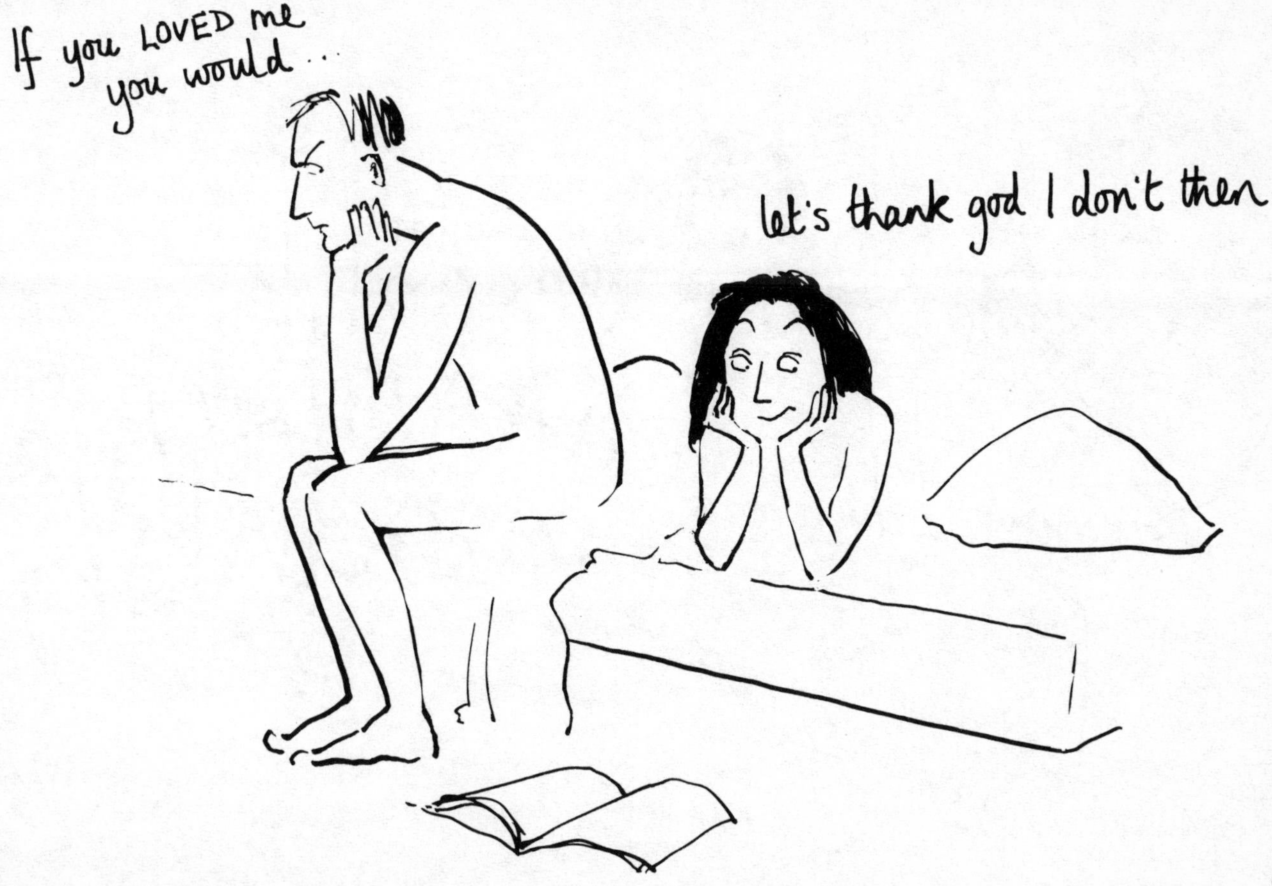
If you LOVED me
you would...
let's thank god I don't then

Romance

From the Latin: pile of old rubbish, romance leads directly to very serious mistakes. It is the real Bad Fairy, the Teller of Whoppas, the Deliberate Deceiver, the Master of Disguises — not to be confused with real magic, wonder, excitement, adventure, and awe, which you will miss whilst SAVING YOURSELF FOR ROMANCE

Sometimes it appears in the form of an Old Bad Fairy who should have been left on a hillside at birth.

you must SAVE yourself for LOVE
...when you find him SURRENDER
to his STRONG embrace....

Romance is not unlike hard drugs –

TEMPORARY HIGH –
followed by grim dishevelled
dissatisfied flat fat ugly
feeling of pointlessness
futility loneliness
disappointment
a bit of a cold
and wanting
MORE of what you
just had which will
give you a
TEMPORARY HIGH –
followed by...

except everyone knows hard drugs are bad for you.

Romance is what makes us **VOLUNTARILY** hoover, cook, iron, shop, change the sheets, change the nappies and generally...

aim to please

To keep us pleasing and .... preoccupied, we are encouraged to

paint our faces

smile more than is necessary

eat less than is necessary

enlarge our breasts

    reduce our breasts

remove our bellies thighs and bottoms

  remove our body hair

diet

    diet

pluck   wax   diet

    SMILE

and shave our legs

because no self-respecting man wants a hairy woman to do his hoovering. And no self-respecting hairy woman would.

and if I make myself incredibly attractive
can I shop and cook for you as well?

if you MUST

Those vague and romantic promises of childhood are finally fulfilled

and iron your shirts
clean the toilet and
take the children to school?

only if you lose weight

and if aiming to please wears a bit thin we think we're probably hoovering for the wrong man until

an almost forgotten memory stirs in our nostrils . . .

This moment of clarity does raise some niggly questions like

am I completely barmy?

and the answer is yes. Completely.

In fact you have successfully achieved exactly what is expected of us — not a lot. Try not to dwell on it.

It is worth bearing in mind that secretly men have always been amazed at what women will do for love, because THEY wouldn't do it for ANY REASON.

Getting Out

You may panic at this point and think that anybody is better than nobody but this is not true.

You may panic at this point . . . .but I repeat myself

75

Try not to undervalue your friends.

They have already watched you shamelessly humiliate yourself

alone again

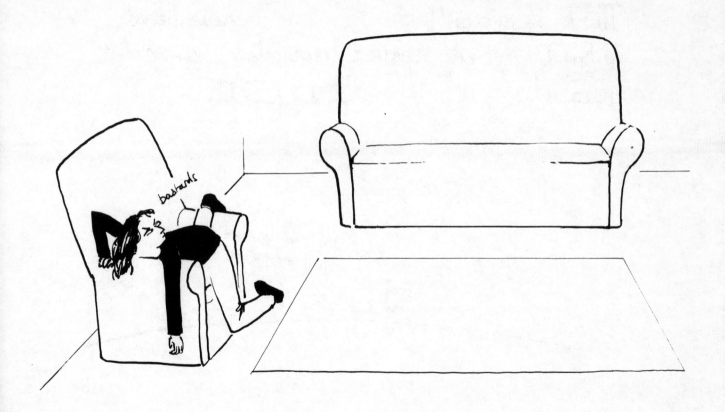

Think of yourself as . . . . unencumbered,
restored, revived, repaired, reinstated, rejuvenated
released, ... FREE

free . . . . free . . . free as a bird . . . .
. . . . . free to do WHATEVER I like . . . .

Please do this in private where no-one can see you.

Don't be in a rush to fall on familiar ground.

Be choosy. Be unreasonable. Be cantankerous. Be foul. Be difficult. But don't, whatever you do, be accommodating.

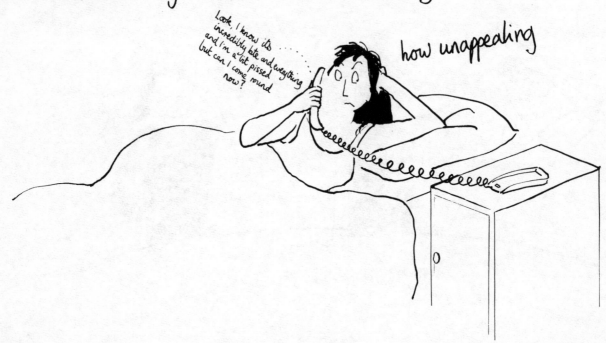

Stop being nice about it. Ask yourself:

have I got time for this (WHY have you?)

is he (perish the thought) a bit of a plonka?

does he think little fairies come and clean the toilet?

do I also find farts extraordinarily funny?

do I really want to pay off his overdraft,
make his sandwiches, cure his drug problem?

Epilogue

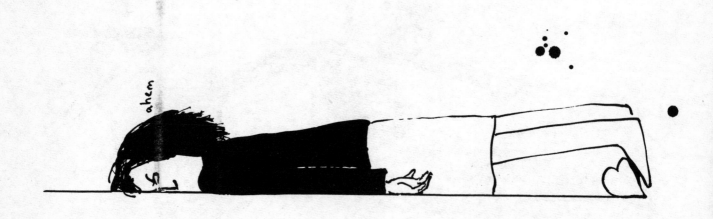

Please turn to page one.